The Hatseller and the Monkeys

Written by Susheila Stone
Illustrated by Andrew Midgley

Collins Educational

The Hatseller came down the road.
"Buy my hats! Buy my hats!" he cried.

On his head he carried a
huge basket, full of hats.

The sun was beating down and
the Hatseller felt very tired.

He lay down under a tree
and fell fast asleep.

Now little did the Hatseller know, but a troop of monkeys lived in that tree. Raju was their leader.

Raju saw the basket of hats.
He climbed down the tree and
grabbed one of the hats.

Raju climbed back up the tree
and put the hat on his head.

Then all the other monkeys,
who had been watching Raju,
climbed down the tree.

They each grabbed a hat and
climbed back up the tree with it.

The monkeys chattered loudly
as they tried on the hats.

All the noise woke the Hatseller.
"Those are my hats!" he cried.
"Give them back!"

He picked up a stone and
threw it at the monkeys.

The monkeys picked berries
from the tree and threw
them at the Hatseller.

The Hatseller shook his fist
at the monkeys.

The monkeys shook their
fists at the Hatseller.

The Hatseller was very puzzled.
He scratched his head.

The monkeys scratched their heads.

"You are copying me!"
cried the Hatseller.

Then he had an idea.
He took off his own hat and
threw it on the ground.

The monkeys took off their hats
and threw them on the ground.

The Hatseller quickly picked up the
hats. He put them in his basket
and ran off down the road as
fast as he could go.